# Webster's
# First
# Phonics

Compiled by Stuart Dent

Edited by Tracey Biscontini

BCL Press • New York

# Contents

Each page of this book shows words with a particular sound.

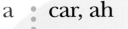

| | |
|---|---|
| a | car, ah |
| air | pair, stare, tear |
| aw | saw, sauce, chalk |
| ay | day, snail, rake |
| b | bat, ball, rabbit |
| ch | cherry, hatch, picture |
| d | dad, puddle |
| e | egg, electric, bell |
| ee | bee, bead, piece |
| f | fork, knife, phone, tough |
| g | girl, frog, ghost |
| h | hat, horn |
| i | insect, pill, crystal |
| igh | light, pine, eye, sky |
| j | jar, orange, bridge |
| k | kitten, cat, block, school |
| ks | box, mix, blocks, jacks |
| l | lemon, blue, shell |
| m | mom, hammer, comb |
| n | nest, bunny, knight |
| o | ostrich, top |
| oa | boat, blow, nose, no |

| | |
|---|---|
| oo (short) | look, wood, pull |
| oo (long) | zoom, fruit, glue, cute |
| or | corn, door, store, warm |
| ow | cow, house |
| oy | toy, coin |
| q | queen, squirt |
| p | peas, top |
| r | rose, car, wrist |
| s | salt, glass, cycle, science |
| sh | shell, brush, vacation |
| t | tail, bat, bottle |
| th | think, both |
| u | umbrella, duck, money |
| v | van, driver |
| w | water, whistle |
| y | yellow |
| z | zip, puzzle, roses |
| endpapers | The alphabet |

Webster's First Phonics was conceived, commissioned and produced by Book Creation, LLC

Compiler: Stuart Dent • Editor: Tracey Biscontini • Managing Editor: Simon Shelmerdine
Picture Research: Joseph Kiley • Book Designer: Kevin McGuinness

Webster's First Phonics © 2002, Book Creation, LLC

Photgraphy: Anatographica, LLC; Belden Hill Picture Library; Church Street Photo Archives; Corbis ®; Corel Corporation; CPG Picture Library; Creativ Collection®; Digital Stock; Photodisc®; PhotoSpin; Plantstock.com; PowerPhotos™

Cover © 2002, Kevin McGuinness
ISBN 0-9710070-3-9
Printed and bound in China

01 02 03 04 LFA 9 8 7 6 5 4 3 2 1

**D**o you remember learning to read? Becoming a competent reader is a process that can take several years. Very young children actually begin learning some of the basics of reading when they listen to people speak. They match spoken words with objects and actions. They communicate with others by saying words. But learning to speak is much more intuitive than learning to read; it involves repetition and recognition, but not an understanding of the complex code that is written language. That code must be taught, and learning it takes time and patience for both parent and child.

**A** Start early and practice often, but for short periods of time. Make discovery fun, and don't expect to accomplish too much at once. If you are frustrated by what seems to be slow progress, your child will know it and share your frustration, making the lesson something to be avoided.

**B** Children learn best when learning is interactive. Interactive learning is "hands on" and usually involves more than one thing. Make learning with this book interactive. Use the tips at the bottom of the pages. When teaching your child a particular sound, go beyond the book and show him or her other objects with that sound. Let your child touch and hold the objects. Young children are concrete learners — they learn best when they can see and touch things.

**C** You can begin familiarizing your pre-reader with the process of learning to read by just looking through the book with him or her. Let your child point to the pictures in the book and name them. Praise your child and make learning to read a positive experience. Go slowly. Work on only a page or two at a time.

**D** Mastering the alphabet is essential for pre-readers. This is the first major step toward reading. Children need to recognize the different letters and grasp the idea that letters make spoken sounds. Learning the alphabet takes time. While you have probably already started teaching your child the alphabet through board books, rhymes, and toys, you can use this book to help strengthen this first step. There is a complete picture alphabet on the inside back cover for quick reference.

**E** Once pre-readers know the alphabet, they're ready to learn the different sounds that letters make. Begin with consonants since they make only one sound. Begin with one or two consonant letters. You'll remember that *b, c, d, f, g, h, j, k, m, n, p, q, r, s, t, v, w, x, z* are consonant letters. The letter *y* is usually considered a consonant as well, although it can make more than one sound.

Turn to a page showing a consonant letter and tell your child the sound that letter makes. Speak clearly. Then ask your child to name each picture on the page. Look at the word next to the picture. Show your pre-reader the letter in the word. For example, if you're teaching the letter *d*, show your child the *d* in *doll* and *dog*; the letter *d* in these words is in a different color to make it easy to spot.

**F** Once you have introduced your pre-reader to consonants, move on to vowels. The vowels— *a, e, i, o,* and *u*—are listed at the bottom of each double–page of *Webster's First Phonics*. Explain to your child in a simple way that some letters make more than one sound. Point out that one of the sounds these letters make is their name—*a* can sound like *a* in *apron* or it can sound like *a* in *apple*. Point out the letters around letters that make more than one sound. For example, show the way that *e* with *a* makes the long *e* sound as in *seat*.

Teach short vowel sounds first since they are easier to master. Avoid using difficult terminology when you explain vowels to your child; Don't say "long a" or "short a." Simply note that some letters make more than one sound. Point out that the letter *a* sounds different in *ant* and *apple* than it does in *play*.

**G** When your child knows the alphabet and the different sounds that the letters make, move on to consonant blends such as *br, cr, dr, fr, gr, pr, tw, wr, bl, cl, fl, gl, pl, sl, scr, str, sm, sn, sp, sc,* and *sk.* You'll find these blends in words pictured throughout the book. Next review digraph sounds, the letter combinations that have their own unique sounds: s*h, ch, th, wh* and *ng.*

Later, move on to the double vowel sounds *ai, ea, ee, oa, ui, oo, ou,* and *ow.* You'll find plenty of examples for these sounds in *Webster's First Phonics.* In time, you can review more complicated sounds with your child such as silent *e.*

**H** Note that while beginning readers may be able to read some words, they may not be able to write them. Young children often don't immediately make the connection between recognizing letters and writing them. Separate practice for learning to comfortably write the alphabet is required.

**I** Remember to keep your sessions short. A young child has only a short attention span. Five or ten minutes is a good length of time for a session. Give your child lots of praise while he or she is learning. Treating this book like a wonderful puzzle can make learning to read fun for your child.

The following are some additional rules about sounds that will help you teach your child to read using *Webster's First Phonics*. These are here as reminders for *you*. Don't have your child memorize too many rules until he or she is truly confident with the letter and word basics. Plenty of repetition will help your child learn these rules in their context, before he or she may be up to applying a rule to a whole range of words.

- When c comes before e, i, or y in a word, it usually makes the s sound as in bicycle.

- When e comes after v and z at the end of a word, it's silent, as in wave and maze.

- When le comes at the end of a word, the letters make the l sound as in little and settle.

- When the letter e comes after ng at the end of a word, it makes the nj sound as in strange.

- When the letter s comes before i, u, or y in the middle of a word, it usually makes the zh or sh sound as in pleasure.

- The digraph wh usually makes the sound as in the word white. However, when it comes before the letter o, the h is silent as in whole.

- When the letter y comes at the end of short word, it usually makes the long i sound as in fly. But in longer words, it usually makes the long e sound as in silly, happy, and friendly.

- When the letters ee, ai, oa, and ay appear in a word, they usually make the long sound of the first vowel, as in see and say.

## Using This Book

- *Webster's First Phonics* is designed to help children learn basic sounds. Very young children can use the book to learn the letters of the alphabet. A complete picture alphabet is printed on the inside back cover for review.

- Each page features a single sound, regardless of the letters that make it.

- The letter/sound featured is shown at the top of the page, along with a sentence underneath telling us something about the sound and the letter or letters that make it.

- Fun, brightly-colored pictures are designed to hold a child's interest.

- Words are grouped within the page by the letters that make the featured sound.

- The letter or letters in the words that make the featured sound are highlighted in color so pre-readers can spot them easily. Some words show the letter at the beginning of a word. Others show the letter in the middle or at the end of the word.

- A "Say and Spell" quiz appears at the bottom of each page.

- Teaching tips at the bottom of the page help make learning interactive.

- Vowels are also listed at the bottom of each double-page spread to help children identify letters that make more than one sound.

# a

a sometimes sounds the way it does in dad, lamp or pal.

cat

jar

carrots

car

hat

parrot

jam

lamb

elephant

cab

rabbits

man

astronaut

cap

woman

glasses

map

_nt    gl_ss

Parent tip: The *ph* in *elephant* is a digraph, a pair of letters that has a unique sound.

a    e    i    o    u

# air

is what we breathe. It also is a sound in many words. Sometimes words with ear or are in them sound the same.

hair

pair

stare

chair

dairy

square

share

snare drum

care

scarecrow

bear

wear

pear

Say and Spell    h___ brush    ___plane

Parent tip: Explain to advanced readers how different spellings that sound alike change meanings, like *pair* and *pear*.

# aw

makes the sound we hear in saw and paw. Listen for the same sound in words with au like sauce or caught, and when a is followed by ll or lk, like call or talk.

yawn

jigsaw

macaw

strawberry

claws

paws

crawl

chalkboard

ball

small

tall

walk

astronaut

laundry

mother & daughter

cup & saucer

Say and Spell        s＿＿

a        e        i        o        u

# ay

together sounds way we say a. It can sound the same way with ai, like nail, or in words where another vowel makes the difference, like late or bake.

pail

daisy

paint

sailboat

snail

aim

grapes

tape

plate

crayon

skate

lazy

shady

tray

lady

play

say

Parent tip: *e* at the end of a word like *plate* or *skate* is silent, but makes vowel before it a long sound.

a     e     i     o     u

# b

b almost always sounds the same, like bread, butter, bubble or cub. Say: bat, boat, buzz, rub, tub.

banana

bandage

baby

blocks

box

tabby

brown cow

rubber ball

butterfly

bowl

bottle

blueberries

bugs

break

butcher

bean

baker

brush

_ee

_oot

Parent tip: When *mb* are together the *b* is silent as in *climb, lamb* or *plumber*.

# ch

together makes the sound we hear in children or stitch. When t is with ure it makes the same sound in words like future or adventure. Say: chalk, choose, much, touch.

chair

chocolate

chess

chimes

chest

cheese

mixture

picture

furniture

creature

vulture

chick • hatch

watch

watches

catch

__erry

__imp

Parent tip: *ch* is another digraph, it always makes the same sound.

# d

d almost always sounds the same, the way it does in deer or food. Say: drop, bed, sled.

daffodil

deer

dirt

ladder

dog

ducky

doll

paddle

dad

drum

desk

ride

bread

dinner

drawing

_uck

Parent tip: A single vowel followed by one or two consonants usually makes the short sound as in *doll*.

a    e    i    o    u

# e

**e** is the letter we use the most. It can sound many different ways, and sometimes doesn't make a sound at all. **E** in the front or middle of a word can sound the way it does in **egg** or **head**.

egg

lemon

dessert

pepper

lettuce

elephant

berries

shell

pen

bell

yell

letters

thread

measure

breakfast

bread

p_t

h_ad

Parent tip: e at the end of a word like ate or wrote is silent but changes the sound of the vowel before it

# ee

A double e in words like knee sounds the way we say its name. The same sound can come from ea in words like eat or meat or ie in piece, and from y at the end of a word like puppy.

trees

sheets

cheese

feet

teeth

peach

ice cream

peanut

meat

leaf

peacock

piece of pizza

lillies

donkey

key

fluffy

puppies

money

Parent tip: When making the plural of a word ending in y, drop the y and add *ies* as in *puppies*.

a    e    i    o    u

# f

f has its own sound like feather, first or frozen. Letter pairs that sound like f are ph, like photo, and sometimes gh at the end of a word, like rough. Say: favor, fish, soft, enough.

farmer

family

fast

fire

furry

fish

full

flower

flour

leaf

flags

flute

knife

calf

frog

half

chef

telephone

alphabet

elephant

tough

_ly

Parent tip: When it's at the end of a short word like *fly*, the letter *y* usually sounds like long *i*.

# g

g almost always sounds the same. Say: Give grandpa a bag of gifts.

gear

gift

glass

girl

gas can

gloves

goggles

grapefruit

greens

gold

grasshopper

grill

dig

frog

wagon

piglet

a     e     i     o     u

# h

h at the start of a word makes a sound like you are breathing out, like ha ha, hat or head.

ham

hatchet

hitchhiker

hamster

hamburger

hen

helmet

hammer

hearts

horse

harp

hot

head

horn

hands

Parent tip: *h* gives up its sound when part of the digraphs *ch*, *sh*, *th* and *wh*.

a    e    i    o    u

# i

is a letter we use a lot. It makes an "eh" sound like it or sit. Listen for this when i is in the beginning or middle of a word, or when y follows c in words like cymbal or bicycle.

ill

insect

rings

king

iguana

inside

starfish

grill

chimp

big pig

milk

film

chick

sewing kit

bicycle

chips

electric guitar

tricycle

p_lls

6

s_x

Parent tip: When the letter i comes after *c*, *sc*, *s*, *ss* or *x*, it makes the *s* sound as in *city*.

# igh

sounds the way we say i, like in high or right. So does i with an e one or two letters after it, like pie or wire, and sometimes y in words like fly or sky.

pie

tie

high chair

knight

fighter

miner

climber

5 five

fireworks

dinosaur

triangle

pinecone

writing

clothesline

ice skate

bite

9

kite

sky

# j

almost always sounds the same like jar or jam or jump. G makes a sound like j in words like orange or large or page.

jack in the box

jar

jigsaw puzzle

janitor

judge

jelly beans

jogger

jump

jewlery

jet pilot

jacks

lumberjack

luggage

orange

Say and Spell

pa_e

_uice

Parent tip: The letters *j*, *k*, *q*, *w*, *x*, and *v* are never doubled.

a     e     i     o     u

# k

k almost always sounds the same way, like it does in kiss or bike. C sounds the same in words like cake and crunch.

cards

cat

car

cookie

kitten

candy

candle

captain

clock

clown

crayons

kiss

duck

king

cup

kangaroo

puck

Say and Spell     _amera          _ey

Parent tip: *ch* before a consonant makes the *k* sound as in *Christmas*.

a     e     i     o     u

# ks

makes the sound we hear in socks, drinks, thinks.
X almost always sounds the same way too, like fox, box or fix.

box

boxing gloves

saxophone

taxi

mixed nuts

wax candle

jacks

blocks

clocks

drumsticks

rubber ducks

drinks

bricks

6

si_     a_

Parent tip: The letter *x* can also make the *z* sound as in *xylophone*.

# 1

almost always makes the same sound, like laugh, love or pull.

lantern

lamb

ladder

lollipop

lemon

lime

leaves

glue

gloves

flower

milk bottle

flashlight

tall

doll

ball

shell

balloon

wheel

snail

nai_

# m

m almost always makes the same sound, like monkey, mommy, ham or Tom.

man

matches

magnet

mask

medicine

marbles

melon

motor

mouse

musician

money

helmet

tomato

hamster

plumber

remote

hammer

comb

gum

Say and Spell _ilk

ha_

Parent Tip: The *b* in *mb* is silent, as in *plumber* and *comb*.

a    e    i    o    u

# n

n almost always sounds the way it does in grandma, no or nice. When k or g come before n, all we hear is the n sound like kneel or gnaw.

nails

nuts

notebooks

needle

nurse

gnome

knitting yarn

knight

knife

pan

gnawing

pine cone

phone

snake

runner

bone

pony

Parent tip: Review other words with *kn* where the *k* is silent: *knob, knock, knot, know,* and *knee.*

a    e    i    o    u

O can gave a soft sound like saying "ah" in words like hop, stop and log. The a in what, was and wash sounds the same.

frogs hop

socket

rocking chair

dog

doll

blocks

clock

soccer ball

rocket

gloves

popcorn

box

pot

chocolate

watch

wash

wasp

# oa

together in words like oats or float sounds the way we say o. So does ow in words like tow or row. Also listen for o the way we say it in words like bone, broke, home or stole.

boat

slow

goat

bow

wheelbarrow

yellow raincoat

hose

funny nose

pinecone

notebooks

rose

tomato

oboe

pony

violin

Say and Spell teleph_ne          b__ tie

Parent tip: When consonants are doubled, in words like fu*nny* and wheelba*rr*ow, only one sound is pronounced.

a          e          i          o          u

# OO

OO sometimes makes a sound like "uh" in words like wood or stood. The same sound comes from u in words like fun or put.

cook

crook

books

wool

look

woof

woodpecker

hood

pin cushion

squirt gun

push

pull

full

Say and Spell    w__d

Parent tip: This sound is called the "short" *o*.

# OO

OO can also make a sound like "ew" in words like cool or pool or with u in words like cute, parachute or flu.

toot

tool

toothbrush

school bus

mushrooms

spoon

shoe

crew

kangaroo

sailor

screwdriver

glue

blueberries

lute

flute

fruit

cucumbers

b__t

Parent tip: This sound is called the "long" o.

a    e    i    o    u

# or

together almost always makes the same sound like in order or more. In many words our and oar can make the same sound too. Say: your, pour, roar, board.

core

corn

doctor

door

motor

seashore

popcorn

lying on the floor

fork

pour

cork

horn

chess board

short

warrior

quarters

roar

4

f___

# OW

ow and ou together can make the sound we hear when we say wow! or ouch! Say: now, plow, ground, pound.

cow

brown hen

owl

looking down

cowboy

clown

shower

flower

flour

round

sour

pout

mouth

shout

Say and Spell

m__se

a    e    i    o    u

# oy

......................

and oi make the sound we hear in words like ahoy, soy, boil and broil. Say: joy, Roy, spoil, toil.

metal foil

oil lamp

point

olive oil

coins

soil

noise makers

cowboy

decoy

royal

toys

annoyed

enjoy

boys

Say and Spell                    b__l

Parent tip: The *s* at the end of *boys* and *toys* sounds like *z*.

# p

p almost always sounds the same when there is a vowel before or after it. Think of peas, potatoes or parrot.

pepper

pot

pear

pony

puppet

pet

puppy

pie

pins

pencil

spider

pen

penguin

spoon

spur

grapes

soap

lamp

tape

Say and Spell

p_ _

Parent tip: When the letter *c* comes before *e, i,* or *y,* it is soft as in *pencil.*

# q

q is almost always followed by u, and makes a sound like the k in kick with the w in water.

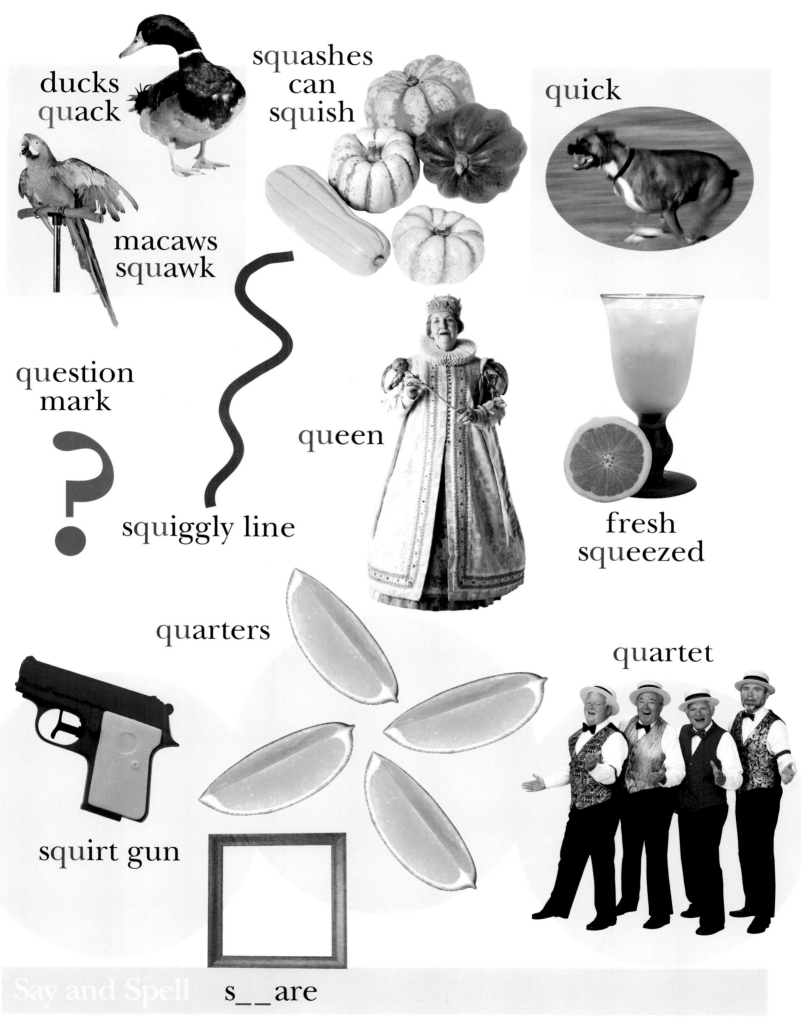

ducks
quack

macaws
squawk

squashes
can
squish

quick

question
mark

squiggly line

queen

fresh
squeezed

quarters

quartet

squirt gun

s__are

a    e    i    o    u

# r

r almost always makes the same sound. Say: race, rip, growl, trip, fur.

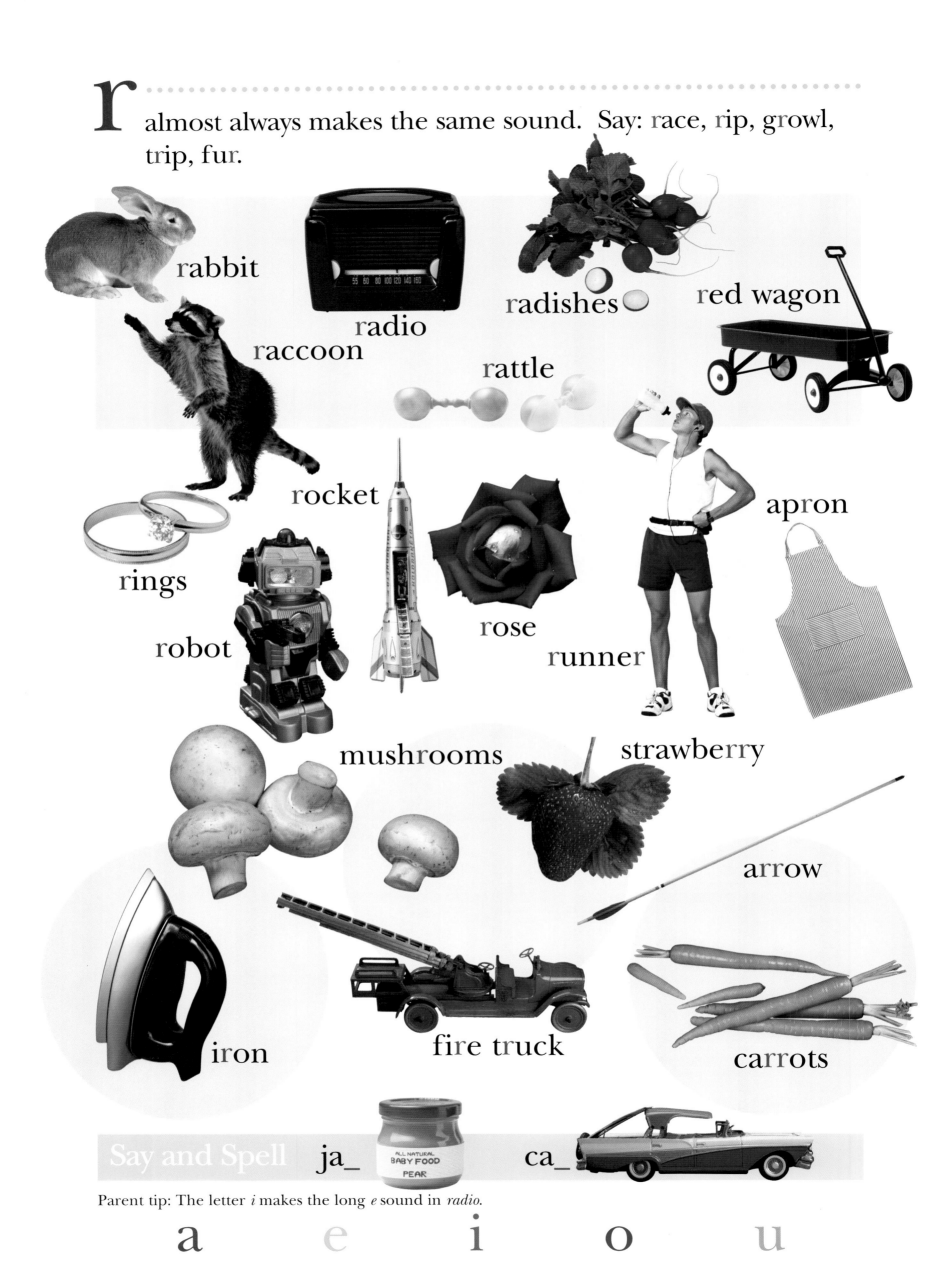

rabbit

radio

radishes

red wagon

raccoon

rattle

rocket

rings

robot

rose

runner

apron

mushrooms

strawberry

arrow

iron

fire truck

carrots

Parent tip: The letter *i* makes the long *e* sound in *radio*.

a    e    i    o    u

# S

**S** almost always sounds the same. When you see s, think of hiss and snake. Ce and cy can make the same sound in words like nice and bicycle. Say: silly, fast, kiss, twice, cymbal.

sailboat

sandcastle

salt

sandwich

scale

seashell

scooter

scarecrow

popsicle

kiss

glasses

bicycle

dancer

center

cereal

tricycle

_oda

Parent tip: The letter *a* before *l* usually makes the *au* or *aw* sound as in *salt*.

# sh

sh ............................................................................................

together almost always sounds the same. When you see sh, think of hush or shush. Say: shave, shoulder, wish, push.

salt shaker

shamrock

shampoo

shell

sheets

ship

shovel

shout

shopper

shoes

dishes

washcloth

cash register

paintbrush

trash

mushrooms

Say and Spell

fi__

# t

t almost always sounds the same, like tap or pat, especially before or after a vowel. Say toe, tree, stop, stick, sit.

tabby

table

teacher

tail

teddy bear

teacup

timer

tin can

tool

tiger

top

toy truck

tulip

turtle

kitten

mittens

hat

bottle

cat

_ape

Parent tip: *le* at the end of a word is pronounced *ul* as in *bottle*, *table* or *turtle*.

a     e     i     o     u

# th

.......... together makes a different sound from t by itself. When you see th, think of thin things. Say: that, there, both, tooth.

thick

thin

throw

thimble

thermometer

thread

through

mouth

3 three

birthday

bathing suit

washcloth

clothes

math

mother

moth

toothbrush

__umb

tee__

Parent tip: The *bl* as in *thimble* is a common consonant blend.

a     e     i     o     u

# u

makes a sound like "uh" in cut, or bump. Sometimes o can sound the same, like in cover or honey. Say: under, up, but, cub, tub, rub, Monday, monkey.

umbrella

bug

upside down

cup

ugly alien

bubbles

lumberjack

cupcake

jump

hug

duck

mushrooms

money

trumpet

pumpkin

puppet

onions

gloves

tr_ck

Parent tip: *u* after *s* or *ss* makes the *zh* sound as in *measure*.

# V

V almost always sounds the same. When you see v think of vases of violets. Say: van, very, visit, love, move.

vacuum cleaner

valentine candy

vegetables

vest

videotape

violin

volleyball

vitamins

seven 7

invitation

caveman

traveler

sky diver

gloves

doves

Say and Spell          _ase

a      e      i      o      u

# W

almost always sounds the way it does in well or water.
Say: wag, want, what, wig.

wagon

water

wave

wedding

weights

wheelbarrow

white bowl

wheat

whip

whiskers

wings

wood

world

woof

woman

sweep

_asp

Parent tip: *w* is silent when it comes before *r* at the beginning of a word as in *write* and *wrist*.

# y

at the start of a word sounds the way is does in yes or yours. Say: yap, yam, yogurt, yoga, yummy.

yacht captain

yawn

yell

yard

young dancer

first year bithday

pointing at you

yucky worm

egg yolk

yo yo

yellow pepper

Say and Spell

_arn

Parent tip: *y* or *ey* at the end of longer words usually make the long *e* sound as in *happy*.

# Z

Z makes a sound like bees buzzing. S can sound the same way, especially near or at the end of a word like in no*s*e or pepper*s*.

zebra

kazoos

wizard

0 zero

lizard

fizzy

buzz

puzzle

doze

cheese

pizza

rose

presents

vase

pose

hose

nose

glasses

pill_

shoe_

Parent tip: *se* sometimes make the *z* sound as in the*se*.

a   e   i   o   u

# The Alphabet

**Aa**

**Bb**

**Cc**

**Dd**

**Ee**

**Ff**

**Gg**

**Hh**

**Ii**

**Jj**

**Kk**

**Ll**

**Mm**